Grammar?
No Problem!

Grammar?
No Problem!

Dave Davies

SkillPath Publications
Mission, Kansas

Project Editor: Kelly Scanlon

Editor: Jane Doyle Guthrie

Cover and Book Design: Rod Hankins

ISBN: 1-57294-080-8

Library of Congress Catalog Card Number: 97-68153

10 9   **05 08 07 06 09**

Printed in the United States of America

Contents

Introduction

First impressions are lasting impressions. It's natural to want to show yourself at your best, all the time. This is especially important in writing.

Writing provides a permanent record of communication. The reader forms an impression of the writer based not only on WHAT is said but also HOW it is said. Use of language is all-important. Sometimes a slip in grammar is all it takes to harm your credibility!

Many of us, realizing the importance of grammar, become nervous about writing. We start to ask ourselves questions like:

- Is that correct?

- Does that sound right?

- Is that "good" or "bad" English?

Self-doubt isn't the answer. It cramps our style, and discourages us from saying what we really want to say, or writing what we really want to write. The best way to build your confidence is to have the answers right at your fingertips!

That's where *Grammar? No Problem!* comes in handy. This book is designed to do three things:

1. Present the **rules** of "good" grammar (the grammar that most writers accept as standard)

2. Point out the **trouble spots** in each area

3. Give you the chance to **exercise** your grammar skills for competent, confident writing

Grammar Basics

Parts of Speech

Understanding grammar requires understanding parts of speech, the eight categories into which words fall according to their use in a sentence:

1. Noun: Names a person, place, or thing
Sally, Germany, house, river, rose

2. Pronoun: Replaces a noun (that is its "antecedent")
I saw your painting.   *It*   *was beautiful.*
   antecedent   pronoun

3. Verb: Expresses action, existence, or occurrence (there are main verbs and auxiliary, i.e., helping verbs)
  main   auxiliary   +   main
I saw you.   *I have*   *seen you.*

4. Adjective: Describes (i.e., modifies) a noun
    adjective   noun
It was a beautiful   *painting.*

5. Adverb: Modifies a verb
    verb   adverb
She paints   *beautifully.*

6. Preposition: Expresses relationships of space, time, and so on between objects or ideas
  object a   preposition   object b
The book   *is*   *on*   *the table.*

7. Conjunction: Joins words or groups of words
Bill *and* Ben
We looked *but* we didn't find it.

8. Interjection: Expresses emotion
Hey! Hah! Oh! Huh? Agh!

Trouble Spots

- Choosing the wrong part of speech, or otherwise using words inappropriately in a sentence.

Exercise

Below is a quotation from a 1928 speech by President Herbert Hoover. Look at each word and decide its part of speech:

"Our country has deliberately undertaken a great social and economic experiment noble in motive and far-reaching in purpose."

1. Our _____

2. country _____

3. has _____

4. deliberately _____

5. undertaken _____

6. a _____

7. great _____

8. social _____

9. and _____

10. economic _____

11. experiment _____

12. noble _____

13. & 17. in _____

14. motive _____

15. and _____

16. far-reaching _____

18. purpose _____

Subject-Verb-Object

- To be complete, a sentence must have a verb. Most sentences also have a subject (the doer of the action) and an object (the recipient of the action).

- Sentences follow these basic patterns:

  A. Subject + verb:
     John   slept.

  B. Subject + verb + direct object:
     The cat   ate   the mouse.

  C. Subject + verb + indirect object + objective complement:
     She   pushed   him   hard.

  D. Subject + verb + indirect object + direct object:
     Sue   lent   me   her pen.

  E. Subject + linking verb + noun or adjective (called a "copula"):
     My mom   is   a lawyer.
     She   seems   happy.

- There are also four important variations to these basic sentence patterns:

  a. Commands (show no subject):
     Stop!

  b. Questions (put an auxiliary verb first):
     Will you come?

  c. Passives (put the object of the action as the subject of the sentence):
     Mice are chased by cats.

  d. Expletives, or "fill-in" words *there* or *it* (put the subject after the verb):
     There is someone at the door. (cf: Someone is at the door.)

Trouble Spots

- Writing incomplete sentences or sentence fragments with no verb:

The other one.

Over the hills and far away.

Exercise

Label the structure of each sentence below with one of patterns A-E, variations a-d, or as "fragments":

Examples:

The one I gave you the other day.   fragment

Goethe was a German writer.   pattern E

1. The boss gave me a raise. _____

2. Fresh water tastes great. _____

3. The thick, heavy clouds descended. _____

4. Are they joining us or not?_____

5. Just hold it right there. _____

6. The harbor has been closed due to pack ice._____

7. Once upon a time. _____

8. You are going to hurt yourself._____

9. They painted the table yellow. _____

10. It was obvious that the Blackhawks would win. _____

Nouns

Proper Nouns

Common noun is the "label" used for a person, place, or thing. A *proper noun* is a name in the official sense. To show the difference, capitalize proper nouns.

- Specific persons:

  Jane, John Stuart Mill

- Specific places:

  Africa, Kansas, Crater Lake, Basin Street

- Historical eras and events:

  the Iron Age, the Boston Tea Party, the Roaring Twenties

- Days of the week, months, holidays, and religious days:

  Monday, January, Thanksgiving, Ramadhan

- Races, peoples, religions, languages:

  Christianity, Allah, Chinese

- Titles and trademarks:

  The Catcher in the Rye, The Wall Street Journal, Pepsi

- Personal titles:

  Professor Higgins, President Chang, Dr. Who

  (Note: The office of President of the United States is always capitalized.)

  Nouns such as *boss, president,* and *department* usually are not capitalized. However, if a specific individual or entity is clearly being referred to, for example when writing about a person *(the Vice President)* or department *(Human Resources)* in your own organization, you may choose to capitalize such words as proper names.

Trouble Spots

- Capitalizing common nouns

  Geese fly *South* in the *Winter*.

  She graduated *University* last *Fall*.

Exercise

Correct the capitalization in the following sentences:

1. On the subject of college, she said she attended stanford in palo alto, california.

2. Around Cree Village there are Rivers, Lakes, and Streams filled with Fish.

3. They said richard was heading for trout lake over hanukkah.

4. The island of manhattan is bounded by the hudson river to the west, the east river to the east, and new york bay to the south.

5. The author of *parks and gardens* is doctor hans helmut gruendaum.

6. Bill was waiting on the North Side of Town with his Father and Brother.

7. The bride-to-be is a german-speaking swiss catholic.

8. Retail Banks like Credit Western normally have their Branches in Malls and on Main Streets.

9. In High School, I enjoyed Sciences, but at Harvard I took a Bachelor of Commerce degree.

10. The liberty bell was commissioned by the pennsylvania state assembly for the state house in philadelphia.

Collective Nouns

- Some nouns, such as *family* or *team*, can be treated as either singular or plural.

If you are writing of the group as a unit, use the singular:
The family is united.

If you are writing of the group as individuals, use the plural:
The staff are worried.

If in doubt, add a term such as *members* and use the plural:
The team members are happy.

Examples of other nouns in this class:

army, navy

board

bunch

committee

corporation

council

crowd

department

faculty

group

herd

jury

majority

police

society

Trouble Spots

- This rule can create some clumsy constructions:

  Corporate America are waiting for the new generation software.

- Don't mix singular and plural forms in the same sentence:

  The faculty has *decided* they *will close the department.*

Exercise

Correct the following singular/plural forms:

1. The company has sworn that they will honor the contract.

2. The committee is close to making a decision, and have in fact expressed a strong interest.

3. Any elected body must shoulder its responsibility to serve their membership.

4. Human Resources have not asked for my advice, so I am sure they can deal with the matter themselves.

5. My family are moving to Rockport, which they think is a better place to live.

6. The board, who are elected by the shareholders, is planning to make some changes.

7. The members of the jury, after long deliberation, has come to its decision.

8. The audience, all of whom must be under fifteen years of age, are going wild.

9. A team that has been properly coached have a better chance of winning the playoffs.

10. It's a firm that dates back to the 1700s, and now they have decided to computerize!

Compound Nouns

- Compounds are two or more words combined to create a new word.
- Some compounds are written as one word:

  masterpiece

- Some are hyphenated:

  trade-off

- Some are written as two words:

  air bag

- Guidelines

  Usually written as one word:

  -down (breakdown)

  -out (handout)

  -over (stopover)

  -back (drawback)

  -away (runaway)

  -about (layabout)

  Usually hyphenated:

  -in (run-in)

  -on (hanger-on)

  rhyming (yo-yo, no-no, culture-vulture)

  phrases of three or more words

Trouble Spots

- Not knowing which of the three categories a compound fits:

  master piece

  tradeoff

  air-bag

Exercise

Following the guidelines, add the compound nouns to the following:

1. I asked for a computer _____ (print + out).

2. The workforce is now facing_____ (cut + backs).

3. Let's get down to the real _____ (nitty + gritty).

4. With all this restructuring, it's like a _____ (merry + go + round).

5. You must have been hungry—there are no _____ (left + overs).

6. The ethics committee has expressed concern about the latest _____ (carryings + on).

7. The authorities have warned of a _____ (crack + down) on demonstrations.

8. I know a little _____ (hide + away) near Monterey.

9. He likes to play the_____ (goody + goody), but I question his motives.

10. The original presenter couldn't make it, so they sent a _____ (stand + in).

Plurals

- The basic rule for forming plurals is to add -s:

  trees, fields, buildings

- Nouns ending in -s, -x, -ch, -sh, or -z form the plural by adding -es:

  losses, boxes, matches, dishes, buzzes

- Nouns ending in consonant + y change to -ies in the plural:

  baby, babies; lady, ladies; party, parties

- Nouns ending in vowel +y mostly form the plural by adding -s:

  boy, boys; guy, guys

- Some older nouns ending in -o form the plural by adding -es:

  echoes, potatoes, tomatoes

- Some newer words and musical terms ending in -o simply add -s:

  commandos, photos, pianos

- Some nouns ending in -f or -fe change to -ves in the plural:

  calf, calves; knife, knives; wife, wives

- Other nouns ending in -f or -fe simply add -s:

  roofs, cliffs, dwarfs

- Some plurals remain the same as the singular:

  sheep, deer, series, headquarters

- Some plurals are entirely new words:

  man, men; mouse, mice; foot, feet; ox, oxen

Trouble Spots

- Trying to form plurals using apostrophes:

  Drink's, hot meal's, and sandwich's

- Using the wrong form of the plural:

  The plane flew low over the village rooves.

Exercise

Give the plurals of the words enclosed in parentheses:

1. There are said to be _____(elf) and _____(witch) in the enchanted forest.

2. Action _____(hero) provide the themes for our new set of _____(logo).

3. Looks like the _____(wolf) have been killing the _____(calf) again.

4. Hair _____(louse) and bad _____(tooth) are typical in conditions of poor sanitation.

5. Audubon identified many new _____(species), especially among _____(goose).

6. The army has separate _____(headquarters) and _____(barracks) for each company.

7. To get to the remote island _____(village), you need to take three _____(ferry).

8. The lifeboat was launched with a cry of "_____(Woman) and _____(child) first!"

9. Although the two _____(watch) look identical, they contain different _____(quartz).

10. I've made several _____(copy) of our new _____(policy).

Plurals From Other Languages

- English is rich in influences from other languages. This can cause confusion when you are forming plurals because borrowed words often form the plural according to the rules of their language of origin.

Following are some common singular and plural endings from other languages:

Singular	Plural	Example
Latin		
-us	-i	radius, radii
-a	-ae	vertebra, vertebrae
-um	-a	memorandum, memoranda
-ix	-es	matrix, matrices
Greek		
-is	-es	basis, bases
-on	-a	criterion, criteria

Trouble Spots

- Anglicizing the plurals of foreign forms indiscriminately (outside the more common ones):

  radiuses, vertebras, criterions

Exercise

Form plurals for the words enclosed in parentheses:

1. Here are our (analysis) of the (datum) you sent.

   _____   _____

2. We have added a number of (matrix) to the (appendix).

   _____   _____

3. The two doctors, fellow (alumnus), came up with differing (prognosis).

   _____   _____

4. As an artist, I use several (medium) to create different (stimulus).

   _____   _____

5. In their (thesis), the scientists put forward two contrasting (hypothesis).

   _____   _____

6. In the desert, you will find (cactus) and (oasis).

   _____   _____

7. Einstein expressed scientific (phenomenon) as mathematical (formula).

   _____   _____

8. Unfortunately, the (bacterium) are causing infection in the (vertebra).

   _____   _____

9. What are the (criterion) for good (memorandum)?

   _____   _____

10. On what (basis) did you make your (diagnosis)?

    _____   _____

Possessives

There are four ways to form the possessive:

- Singular noun not ending in -s, add -'s:

  Claudia and her car, Claudia's car

- Singular noun ending in -s:

  If the possessive can be heard as a separate syllable, add -'s:

  Brutus and his brother, Brutus's brother

  If the possessive is not pronounced as a separate syllable, add an apostrophe only:

  Rutherford Hayes and his presidency, Rutherford Hayes' presidency

- Regular plural noun ending in -s, add apostrophe only:

  the boys and their toys, the boys' toys

- Irregular plural noun not ending in -s, add -'s (as if singular):

  the oxen and their feed, the oxen's feed

  the mice and their cheese, the mice's cheese

Trouble Spots

- Using a plural form instead of a singular possessive:

  Learn how to assure your families income.

- Following the regular rule for irregular plurals:

  the childrens' room

Exercise

Rewrite the following phrases as possessives:

1. the sons of Mr. and Mrs. Jones _____

2. issues concerning women _____

3. the parks and gardens of Paris _____

4. the captains of the ferries _____

5. the interests of the investors _____

6. the offices of the attorneys _____

7. the decision of the executives _____

8. the hills of Arkansas _____

9. the feet of the sheep _____

10. the restaurant of Alice _____

11. the neighborhood of Mr. Rogers _____

12. the locker room of the men _____

13. the highways of California _____

14. the friends of Max _____

15. the soldiers of the corps _____

Compound Noun Possessives

- Compound noun plurals and possessives can be confusing:

Singular	Possessive	Plural	Possessive
son-in-law	*son-in-law's*	*sons-in-law*	*sons-in-law's*
jack-in-the-box	*jack-in-the-box's*	*jack-in-the-boxes*	*jack-in-the-boxes'*

The first pattern normally occurs only when the first part of the compound is a title or action:

pushers-in, passersby, editors in chief

- To form the possessives of compound nouns, follow the rules for other possessives:

singular add -'s:

the vice president's car

plural ending in -s add apostrophe only:

shareholders' options

plural not ending in -s add -'s:

the mothers-in-law's gathering

Trouble Spot

- Using too many possession markers:

my father's-in-law's farm

Exercise

Give the possessive forms for the following:

1. the testimony of the eyewitness

_____

2. the wives of the brothers-in-law

_____

3. the meeting of congresswomen

_____

4. a gathering of culture-vultures

_____

5. the duties of a go-between

_____

6. the comments of passersby

_____

7. the life of a layabout

_____

8. the offices of attorneys-at-law

_____

9. the luck of an old so-and-so

_____

10. the speech of the president-elect

_____

Pronouns

Pronoun and Antecedent

- To avoid repeating nouns, after the first mention, use a pronoun. The noun that a pronoun replaces is called the pronoun's *antecedent*.

antecedent   **pronoun**

    Derek   *locked the door before*   *he*   *left.*

- Pronoun and antecedent must agree in gender and in number.

    Jamal reviewed his notes before the meeting.

    Dogs and cats show their loyalty in many ways.

- Use a plural pronoun if there is more than one singular antecedent joined by *and:*

    Bill and Ben *say* they *are flower-pot men.*

- Use a singular pronoun when the antecedent includes:

any-	-one	either/or
every-	-thing	neither/nor
some-	-body	one
no-		another

    Either *Bill* or *Ben left* his *tools behind.*

- Use a plural pronoun if the antecedent includes *many, few, several, others,* or *both.*

Trouble Spots

- Errors of pronoun number:

    Not one of them know *what they are supposed to do.*

- Separating pronoun from antecedent causes confusion:

    The Dodgers tied with the Giants, even though they *are a better team.*

Exercise

Correct the pronouns in these sentences:

1. Neither Tom, Dick, nor Harry has received their orders yet.

2. Both Sue and Joan knows how to take care of her vehicle.

3. When Jane visited her mother, she had a cold.

4. Either Smith or Jones is going to lose their promotion over this.

5. She changed from medicine to law because it's more demanding.

6. I heard that both Apple and IBM launched its new software.

7. Al and Pete went to the station, where he caught a train.

8. The Blues tied with the Reds—they're a great team!

9. Neither of the campaigns did as well as they were supposed to.

10. The results impressed the directors, since they created new jobs.

Personal Pronouns

PERSON &   **CASE**
NUMBER

	Subjective	Objective	Possessive	Reflexive
Singular				
First person	I	me	my	myself
Second person	you	you	your	yourself
Third person	she	her	her	herself
	he	him	his	himself
	it	it	its	itself
Plural				
First person	we	us	our	ourselves
Second person	you	you	your	yourselves
Third person	they	them	their	themselves

Grammar? No Problem!

Trouble Spots

- Confusing subjective and objective pronouns:

  Jack and me went fishing.

  They invited *Jack and I.*

  If in doubt, separate:

  Jack went fishing and I went fishing.

  They invited Jack and they invited me.

- Misusing the reflexive pronoun:

  For more information, please call Jack or myself.

  (*Myself* can only apply to something *I* do.)

- Using gender-exclusive language:

  Every man has his price.

  (Look for alternatives, e.g., *All people have a price.*)

- Using *it's* (contraction of *it is*) for pronoun *its:*

  The cheetah shifted it's gaze to the family of gazelles.

Exercise

Correct the following with the appropriate personal pronouns:

1. Get yourself a cup of coffee, and bring one for myself.

2. Mary and me went down to the mall.

3. Jack was always rude to the boss, and he wasn't very pleasant to Bert and I either.

4. Before he gives a diagnosis, a doctor should seek a second opinion.

5. Julie is looking happy with Julie, and I would say Julie has had a great day!

6. It was me who told them the news.

7. A human being can't help but put himself first.

8. Between you and I, I think this company is headed for trouble.

9. Bob, Ted, Carol, and myself are all going to the beach party.

10. You saved you and your sister's life.

11. The lodger came in and just helped hisself to the food.

12. A good dog always recognizes it's owner.

13. You people take care of yourself and we'll take care of ourself.

14. Him and her were always fighting, and I knew they weren't doing theirself any good.

15. It's people like they who give all of ourselves a bad name.

Relative Pronouns

- *Who, which,* and *that* are relative pronouns:

  Was the man who shot Liberty Vallance hung?

  The size of the debt, which originally worried me, is shrinking steadily.

  The book that I read on the plane was a fascinating mystery.

- *Who* is used for people. *Which* is used for things (*which* in nonrestrictive clauses, *that* in restrictive clauses).

- *Who* and *which* are also interrogative pronouns:

  Who called?

  Which one did you want?

Trouble Spots

- Using *that* in place of *who* for specific persons:

  the man that shot Liberty Vallance

- Separating the pronoun from the antecedent:

  The book was interesting that I just read.

- Omitting the pronoun completely.

  It was Bill said it.

- Using *that* and *which* interchangeably:

  The car which I bought when I moved to Seattle lasted only two years.

  My silk dress, that I never liked, had to be dry cleaned.

- Using *who* in place of *that* for things or entities:

  Businesses who treat their employees well will thrive.

Exercise

Correct the pronouns in the following:

1. Pat is the only clerk that can be trusted.

2. People which live in glass houses shouldn't throw stones.

3. The dog who bit the mail carrier was destroyed.

4. Don asked for his old job back, that surprised everybody.

5. She is the kind of person which always causes trouble.

6. Their latest record, that I told you about last week, is in the stores.

7. That is a story what is too sad for words.

8. Did you hear of the *Starship Enterprise*, who boldly went where no man had gone before?

9. The person which you suggested proved ideal for the job.

10. It was *The Daily Planet* who first reported the big story.

Who/Whom

- As a relative or interrogative pronoun, *who* is the *subjective* case, *whom* is the *objective:*

Interrogative
Subject:	*Who did it?*
Object:	*Whom shall I say is calling?*
With a preposition:	*To whom did you address it?*
	About whom was she talking?
	With whom was he dealing?
	For whom were they working?

Relative
Subject:	*The person who just left won't be back.*
Object:	*The man whom you mentioned is quite a success.*

- Use *whoever/whomever* when the pronoun relates to a person or persons unknown:

Subject:	*Whoever said that, it isn't true.*
Object:	*Whomever you choose, it's fine by me.*

Note: In modern English, *whom* and *whomever* are often ignored:

Who quoted who?

Choose whoever you want.

Trouble Spot

- Not differentiating between *who/whom* when speaking, and especially when writing, to someone who considers it necessary.

Exercise

Fill in the blanks using *who/whom/whoever/whomever,* as appropriate:

1. To _____ it may concern:

2. The policy becomes payable on death, _____ the beneficiary.

3. A child _____ is in school and _____ earns less than $5,000 is a dependent.

4. Attribution rules apply to loans to people with _____ the taxpayer does not deal at arm's length.

5. If you have children _____ are expected to attend college, you need an education plan.

6. You may nominate _____ you wish as your executor, but it should be someone _____ you trust and _____ is able to take on the responsibility.

7. The settler is the person ____ establishes the trust, the trustees are the parties to _____ the money is entrusted, and the beneficiaries are the persons for _____ the trust is established.

8. Cleopatra and Helen of Troy were women over _____ wars were fought.

9. _____ signed for the shipment, and by _____ was it authorized?

10. "_____ shall I invite?"

   "Invite _____ you wish."

Whose/Who's

- *Whose* is the possessive form of *who.*

  My boss is a person whose insights are uncanny.

- *Who's* is the contracted form of *who is* or *who has:*

  The supervisor who's most likely to get promoted is my boss.

Trouble Spots

- Confusing whose and who's:

  Show me someone whose *got a faster car than mine!*

  Joan is a manager who's *effectiveness is beyond question.*

Exercise

Fill in Whose or Who's as appropriate in the spaces below:

1. _____ drawers were left unlocked?

2. _____ taking out the garbage this time?

3. _____ turn did you say it was?

4. _____ never been to Kansas?

5. _____ car are we taking, by the way?

6. _____ clothes are those lying on the floor?

7. _____ that girl I saw you walking to school with?

8. _____ got a good suggestion for a party this weekend?

9. _____ voice did I hear in the background when you called?

10. _____ the radio mystery person this week?

Verbs

Subject-Verb Agreement

- A verb must agree with its subject in number and person:

  a bird flies, birds fly

- Use a plural verb if there is more than one singular subject joined by *and:*

  Bill and Ben are longtime neighbors.

- Use a singular verb if singular subjects are joined by *or:*

  Mom or Grandpa usually does the shopping.

- Use a singular verb when the antecedent includes:

any-	-one	either
every-	-thing	neither
some-	-body	one
no-		another

  Neither of them knows what's going on.

- Use a plural verb if the subject includes *many, few, several, others,* or *both.*

Note: Phrases like *pitch and toss, bacon and eggs,* which always appear as a unit, normally take a singular verb.

Trouble Spots

- Errors of number and person:

  None of them know what to do.

Exercise

Complete the following with *is* or *are:*

1. One of our planes _____ missing.

2. Everybody _____ invited to the party.

3. Anything and everything _____ for sale.

4. Many _____ called but few _____ chosen.

5. Quantity not quality _____ what we are looking for.

6. Both Smith and Jones _____ being promoted.

7. The cold chicken _____ for lunch.

8. This movie, like most action thrillers, _____ not for children.

9. Mary is one of those people who _____ always active.

10. Be careful! A pair of scissors _____ lying on the chair.

Tenses

- *Tense* shows the time of an action.

- *Aspect* shows whether the action is complete or in progress.

- English has a complex system of tense and aspect combinations:

	ASPECT	
TENSE	**Simple**	**Progressive**
	(fixed/complete)	*(temporary/in progress)*
present	I consider	I am considering
past	I considered	I was considering
future	I will consider	I will be considering
present perfect	I have considered	I have been considering
past perfect	I had considered	I had been considering
future perfect	I will have considered	I will have been considering
future intentional	I am going to consider	I am going to be considering

I have been considering is therefore an example of the *present perfect progressive*.

Trouble Spots

- Not knowing the tenses.

- Confusing the perfect tenses.

The most common error in the use of tenses is confusion of the past perfect and present perfect. For example, you might hear:

"You had mentioned there would be a meeting . . ."

However, that sentence actually implies that something else happened subsequently. For example, *". . . before the phone went dead."*

A better phrasing would be:

"You mentioned there would be a meeting . . ."

Exercise

Identify the underlined tenses in these sentences:

1. By the time <u>we reach</u> Phoenix, <u>I will have been flying</u> for ten hours.

2. We <u>have never seen</u> a more perfect rose.

3. She <u>will be calling</u> on us tomorrow.

4. <u>I came, I saw, I conquered.</u>

5. They <u>will have finished</u> the job by the time <u>we return</u> from lunch.

6. He <u>has been working</u> on this problem for years.

7. I <u>was dancing</u> with my darling when the <u>lights went</u> out.

8. <u>Will you</u> join me? <u>I'll wait.</u>

9. <u>I'm still waiting!</u>

10. He <u>had heard</u> about the Loch Ness monster but he <u>had never seen</u> it.

Sequence of Tenses

- English requires that certain tenses follow each other in a certain order:

past   **present perfect**

My description was sketchy because I have seen her only once.

past   **past perfect**

Before we met yesterday, I had seen her only once.

present   **present perfect**

Although I live next door, I have seen her only once.

- When quoting what somebody said, the tense generally shifts one step into the past:

"I'm leaving"; She said she was *leaving.*

"I've never seen one of these"; He said *he had never seen* one of those.

Trouble Spot

- Shifting from one sequence of tenses to another in midstream:

When I started talking, I was for the bill; but the longer I talked, the more I know I'm against it.

Exercise

Correct the tenses in the sentences below:

1. I thought I will see you at the game.

2. Did you know there is a new store in town, and do you also know they have a sale this weekend?

3. When I asked him where he was going, he said he is going to the mall.

4. The more I sat here, the less interested I become.

5. When the door opened, they see a stranger who asks them for the money.

6. The people were glad to see Bill back at work and wonder where he has been.

7. It was too noisy at home to study. My brother plays guitar, my sister sings, and my dad was vacuuming.

8. My roommate Sharon loves shrimp, so we ate it every evening.

9. When the cougar was captured, it lay quiet, but soon it starts to howl.

10. I've never heard of that movie until you mentioned it yesterday.

Parts of Verbs

- There are three principal parts of a verb:

	Present	Past	Past Participle
Regular			
	I walk	we walked	she has walked
Irregular			
	go	went	gone
	hide	hid	hidden
	rise	rose	risen
	sink	sank	sunk
	split	split	split
	tear	tore	torn

Trouble Spots

- Confusing or using the wrong form of past tense and past participles:

We'd rose early.

He must have went before dawn.

I swum for an hour, then sat on the beach.

Exercise

Supply the correct past participles in the following:

1. I'm nervous—I've never sang in public before.

2. Honey, I shrunk the dogs.

3. He's ran in several relay races.

4. My ears is froze, my nose is froze, and my toes is froze.

5. She's never rode a horse in her life.

6. We'd never spoke to each other until last week.

7. He's wrote them numerous letters but received no replies.

8. They went places they'd never went before.

9. We've gave him plenty of chances to improve his timekeeping.

10. After they had showed us the new product, we were very impressed.

Passives

- The passive *voice* turns the object of the action into the subject of the sentence:

  Active: *John saw Mary.*

  Passive: *Mary was seen by John.*

- The passive construction can dispense with the actor completely:

  Mary was seen.

Note: This is ideal for scientific and technical writing, where actions matter—experiments, processes, and so on—not those who carry them out.

Trouble Spots

- Using the passive with verbs that do not take an object (intransitive verbs):

  I am slept.

- Applying the construction to transitive verbs that do not work in the passive voice:

  A long bath was had by Liz.

- Using the passive voice excessively:

  The party was given for the twins, who had been brought to the house by Graham, and a good time was had by all.

Exercise

Transform the following into the passive:

1. The accident seriously injured her.

_____

2. Someone was following me.

_____

3. Whom are you going to tell about the reorganization?

_____

4. We will have finished everything by Friday.

_____

5. I knew why they had chosen me.

_____

Transform these into the active:

6. It is intended by us to replace you.

_____

7. You were expected earlier by them.

_____

8. They will be disciplined by the principal.

_____

9. Robert has been notified of his dismissal by the personnel manager.

_____

10. Suzie will have been given her present from the gang by now.

_____

Conditionals

- Conditional sentences consist of an "if clause" and a "result clause":

  If you eat your vegetables, you grow up big and strong.

- Some conditional sentences describe situations that are *true* in the *present/future:*

  If I have time, I make my bed in the morning.

  If I have time, I will make my bed in the morning.

  The verb forms here are simple present in the "if clause" and simple present or simple future in the "result clause."

- Some conditional sentences describe situations that are *untrue* in the *present/future:*

  If I had enough time this morning, I would make my bed. *(In truth I don't have enough time, so I won't make my bed.)*

  The verb forms in this construction are simple past in the "if clause" and *would* + simple form in the "result clause."

- Some conditional sentences describe situations that are *untrue* in the past.

  If I had had enough time, I could have made my bed yesterday.

  The verb forms here are past perfect in the "if clause" and *could have* + past participle in the "result clause."

Trouble Spots

- Using *would of* for *would have:*

  It would of worked if you'd of been more careful.

- Using *would have* in the "if clause":

  It would have worked if you would have been more careful.

Exercise

Correct the following conditional forms:

1. If you would not have called, I would not have met you.

2. If she had worked harder, she had passed the exam.

3. They could have won the contest if they'd have had a full team.

4. The town would of been a better place if she'd a been voted mayor.

5. If you asked me, I would have given you the unadulterated truth.

6. Would it be all right if I would bring a partner to dinner?

7. Don't tell me what you woulda, coulda, or shoulda done!

8. If he'd have been ready, you would've never have caught him unawares.

9. Given a bit more time, we would have had completely finished the job.

10. If they had upheld the law, they had not have gone to jail.

Grammar? No Problem!

Subjunctives

- The subjunctive *mood* is the correct grammatical form in sentences that express a wish or recommendation, a supposition, or a condition contrary to fact:

  I insist that she be present.

  A healthy tree would bear fruit.

  It is essential that every employee receive equal benefits.

- The subjunctive often occurs after *if* or *that:*

  If she were tall enough, she could reach the top shelf.

  School policy mandates that each basketball team member have at least a 2.5 GPA.

- The subjective changes *am, are,* and *is* to *be:*

  Protocol demanded that he be seated to my left.

- The subjunctive changes *was* to *were:*

  If Mariah were fully rested, she'd look more alert.

- The subjunctive causes third person verb forms to drop the terminal *-s:*

  I recommend that every teenager take a summer job.

Trouble Spots

- Using the indicative form when the subjunctive is preferable or required:

  I insist that she is present.

  If the tree was healthy, it would bear fruit.

  It is essential that every employee receives equal benefits.

Exercise

Correct the following subjunctive sentences:

1. It is imperative that the information is provided at once.

2. We felt it was important that you came at the earliest opportunity.

3. They insist that he does the work himself.

4. He wishes he was going with you.

5. I demand that we are allowed to speak at the meeting.

6. If only it was my decision.

7. It is the sentence of this court that Briggs remains in prison.

8. The workers requested that they were allowed a pay increase.

9. We recommend that the court awards Mr. Jones punitive damages.

10. Peace should be with you.

Split Infinitives

- An infinitive consists of *to* + the present form of a verb:

  to live, to ride, to love, to be

- When an adverb falls between *to* and the verb itself, the result is called a *split infinitive:*

  To really be, or to merely be?

Note: Split infinitives used to be regarded uniformly as bad grammar, but most experts have become more tolerant of them, particularly in informal writing.

Trouble Spots

- Recognizing when it's all right (or even preferable, to maintain the meaning or balance of a sentence) to split an infinitive:

  She prefers to just talk about problems rather than solve them.

  The managers decided to really go all out in their efforts to improve morale.

Exercise

Correct the split infinitives in the sentences below:

1. We tried to carefully reassemble the parts.
2. Try to, if you can, exercise two or three times every week.
3. They began to gradually pick up the pieces.
4. You ought to thoroughly question the people responsible.
5. I intend to personally supervise the renovations.
6. These figures need to meticulously be checked.
7. The new mare wants to constantly be fed carrots.
8. Tell them to rapidly gather the information.
9. It was impossible to even find one person who was willing to help.
10. We want to really understand what you're trying to say.

Shall/Will

- In American usage, *shall* historically was preferred to indicate future actions or willingness in the first person:

  I shall represent my team at the conference.

  We shall make the changes you suggested.

- *Will* was used to indicate futurity and willingness or expectations for the second and third persons:

  You will miss the kickoff.

  They will never know where to find us.

- Today most writers use *will* for all three persons except for questions and requests where *shall* still prevails in first person question forms:

  Shall I come? Shall we go?

- *Should* and *would* are past forms of *shall* and *will*.

  Both can be used in reported speech:

  "I shall go"; I said I should go.

  "I will go"; I said I would go.

  Should is used in the subjunctive mood:

  If you should go, be sure to take this with you.

  Would is used in polite requests, as a less insistent form of will:

  Would you help me, please?

  Should is frequently used to show obligation:

  It's getting late, so I should go.

Trouble Spots

- Confusing *will* and *shall* in an effort to sound "formal":

  They shall arrive tomorrow night, I believe.

Exercise

Complete the following with the correct form of *will/shall/would/should:*

1. We're leaving now. _____ you meet us there?

2. You _____ report the loss of that key in case there's a security risk.

3. In his youth, he _____ swim a mile every day.

4. _____ you help me, please? I seem to be stuck.

5. I see you have some mail ready to go. _____ I drop it in the mailbox for you?

6. If I _____ fail, remember only that I tried.

7. You could get a promotion, if only you _____ apply yourself.

8. If we had the chance to do it again, _____ we?

9. When confronted, the minister _____ only say "No comment."

10. As a pupil in my class, you _____ do as I say!

Can/May

- *Can* and *could* imply ability.

- *May* and *might* imply possibility and permission.

- *Could* and *might* are less definite than *can* and *may*.

- *Could* and *might*, being past forms, are used in reported speech:

  "I can't jump"; He said he couldn't jump.

  "I may go"; She said she might go.

- *May* is reserved for requests and expressions of hope:

  May I have a cookie?

  May they live happily ever after.

Trouble Spots

- Using *can* for *may* when asking permission:

  "Can I have candy?"

  "I'm sure you can, but you may not!"

- Using *might* alone to talk about past possibilities:

  I saw something last night which might be *a ghost.* (Instead of *might have been a ghost*)

Exercise

Correct the following applications of *can/could/might/may*:

1. Try as I may, I could not get the door open.

2. Can we join you for dinner?

3. Might the happy couple enjoy their new life together.

4. You too can own this car if you had a big enough deposit.

5. They asked if they can come to the zoo, and Dad said they might.

6. When asked, she said she can prepare the report but not before Friday.

7. Why did you play on the street? You may have hurt yourself.

8. There were heavy footsteps and a knock at the door. It might be the police.

9. They asked if we can help them.

10. If you went to bed for a while, you may feel better.

Lay/Lie

- *Lay* and *lie* are not simply different forms of the same word; they are two distinct words with separate meanings. The same goes for *raise* and *rise*.

	Present Participle	Past Tense	Past Participle
lay	laying	laid	laid
lie	lying	lay	lain
raise	raising	raised	raised
rise	rising	rose	risen

- Lay and raise are transitive; that is, they need an object:

	object
I will lay	*the carpet.*
They tried to raise	*the Titanic.*

- *Lie* and *rise* are intransitive—they do not take an object:

  I lay on the grass.

  She rose early that day.

Trouble Spots

- Confusing when to choose *lay* versus *lie:*

  No sooner did I lay down but the phone rang.

  I laid on Baby Bear's bed.

Exercise

Fill in the blanks with the correct form of *lie/lay* or *raise/rise:*

1. Maverick _____ his cards on the table.

2. _____ on the couch, and the doctor will be here in a moment.

3. I _____ myself early to get a good start on the day.

4. The patient's heart rate has _____ sharply.

5. When _____ carpets, be sure to measure accurately.

6. Scouts were sent ahead to see how the land _____.

7. Certain questions have been _____ that need careful answers.

8. How many eggs has your goose _____ so far?

9. After the race, she _____ still for a long time.

10. The council has _____ the money to _____ ten miles of new pavement.

Negatives

- To make a sentence negative, use only one negative expression:

  I didn't say anything.

- As in mathematics, two negative expressions make a positive:

  I didn't say nothing. (I had to say something.)

  None of the delegates had no opinion on the issue.

Trouble Spots

- Using two negatives when you only need one:

  I'm sorry, I couldn't do nothing *about it.*

Exercise

Correct the use of negatives in the following sentences:

1. They have never had no children.
2. We didn't have no time left.
3. He never hardly comes to visit.
4. You don't have no right to interfere.
5. The company never has no hesitation in firing latecomers.
6. I didn't manage to get the books nor the stationery you requested.
7. They were unable to give us no directions to the ballpark.
8. Bill was not unaware of the situation, so how could he have prevented it?
9. I can't find neither the file nor any other record of this case.
10. Neither trucks nor cars aren't allowed in the city center.

Contractions

- Contractions are formed by fusing two words (sometimes the subject and auxiliary verb; sometimes the auxiliary verb and *not*). The missing letters are indicated by an apostrophe:

  I'm, can't, he'll, she'd, doesn't, you've, there's, we're

Note: Some experts frown on contractions as too informal in writing. However, informality does create a relaxed, friendly tone, which may be appropriate and desirable in certain documents.

Trouble Spots

- Using *whose* for *who's:*

  He's the candidate whose from our district.

- Using *its* for *it's*

  Its about time for annual performance reviews.

- Using *there* or *their* for *they're:*

  Their headed to the mountains.

- Using *your* for *you're:*

  Your my choice for the new committee seat.

- Using *theirs* for *there's:*

  Can you imagine why theirs a need for discussion on this?

Exercise

Construct contractions in the following sentences:

1. I had had enough of the pep talk.

2. You have been very helpful.

3. She would be wise to avoid walking home alone this late.

4. He will see you first thing in the morning.

5. It is a good thing you called me.

6. We are in the process of moving.

7. We had heard rumors about a new campaign.

8. It might not be a bad idea to call first.

9. There is good news, and there is bad news!

10. If we had been given more time, there would be a better chance of success.

11. Do not think you are out of trouble yet.

12. If you could not contribute, why did you not leave well enough alone?

13. Should you not be asking why they were not available?

14. I would not worry; they will have been taking good care of business.

15. I cannot, I will not, and I shall not cooperate with you!

Modifiers

Adjectives Versus Adverbs

- An adjective is a word, phrase, or clause that modifies a noun:

  a *happy* person

  a person *with a happy life*

  a person *who enjoys life to the fullest*

- An adverb is a word, phrase, or clause that modifies a verb, an adjective, or another adverb:

  to try *hard*

  to try *with all your might*

  to try *harder than you have ever tried before*

Trouble Spots

- Using an adjective in place of an adverb:

  I'm doing good.

- Using adjectives out of order:

  a fat little silly dog

- Using too many adverbs:

  Thankfully we've eventually totally gotten rid of them finally.

Exercise

Identify whether each underlined word is an adjective or an adverb:

1. Do you think that was <u>fair</u>? _____

2. I believe the judge ruled <u>fairly</u>. _____

3. The trucker drove <u>hard</u>, all night long. _____

4. The bed was as <u>hard</u> as a rock. _____

5. I can <u>hardly</u> hear you. _____

6. With some <u>quick</u> thinking we might solve this puzzle._____

7. If we don't move <u>quickly</u>, we'll be in trouble. _____

8. The driver stopped <u>short</u>. _____

9. You'll be hearing from us <u>shortly</u>. _____

10. It must be a <u>short</u> circuit. _____

Order of Adjectives

- When more than one adjective is used, they must appear in a specific order, dictated by the following criteria:

evaluation	size	age	color	origin	material
a beautiful	big	old	black	Bohemian	burlap

purpose	noun
betting	purse

Trouble Spot

- Using adjectives out of sequence:

  a modern, big, concrete, nice house

Exercise

Reorder the adjectives as needed in the following:

1. a German, small, beer, brown bottle

_____

2. the greasy, green, great Limpopo River

_____

3. the Pasadena, old, little, delightful lady

_____

4. a dining, oak, round, massive table

_____

5. steel, flexible, thin, long poles

_____

6. a refreshing, cool, long, delicious drink

_____

7. dancing, leather, Italian, white shoes

_____

8. farm, duck, fresh, large eggs

_____

9. a rustic, old, little, remote cottage

_____

10. that Brazilian, splendid, red, big parrot

_____

Compound Adjectives

- Like other compounds, adjectives can be formed of two or more words functioning as a single unit:

  high-pressure sales

  up-to-date information

  well-behaved children

  As a general rule, all elements in a compound adjective are hyphenated.

- Use an en dash in place of a hyphen when one of the elements in the compound is "open" (e.g., New York, Civil War):

  New York–style cab driver

  Civil War–era uniforms

  St. Louis–Los Angeles commute

- An en dash is also preferable when two or more of the elements in the compound adjective are themselves hyphenated compounds:

  Was there a pre–Edwardian—post–Victorian period of fashion?

Trouble Spot

- Knowing where to place the hyphen:

  eighteen year-old daughter

Exercise

Transform the following phrases into nouns preceded by compound adjectives:

Example: a son who is fifteen years old

       <u>a fifteen-year-old son</u>

1. a moment that is never to be forgotten _____

2. a representation in three dimensions _____

3. an affair that is off and on _____

4. information that is off the record _____

5. transactions at the point of sale _____

6. an experience that comes once in a lifetime _____

7. a relationship of cause and effect _____

8. service that is available 24 hours a day _____

9. a journey of ten million miles _____

10. a show comprising a dog and a pony _____

Use of Adverbs

- Adverbs that modify verbs answer questions of *when, where, why,* and *how:*

  Steve showed up on time.

  The wagon train headed west.

  The toddler broke her toy accidentally.

  My assistant faces every task determinedly.

- Adverbs can modify adjectives and other adverbs as well as verbs:

  Eva was too heavy for the fragile chair.

  The message came very late.

- Most adverbs are formed by adding *-ly* to adjectives:

  quick, quickly

  easy, easily

- Some words ending in *-ly* serve as both adjectives and adverbs without any changes:

  The early bird gets the worm.

  I like to arrive early for my appointments.

Trouble Spots

- Trying to change some adjectives ending in *-ly* into adverbs:

  He grinned sillily.

- Placing an adverb between a verb and its object:

  She writes well letters.

- Using adverbs excessively:

  Hopefully, they should probably get here really quickly.

Exercise

Correct the use of adverbs in the following:

1. CompuShop has some real good deals this week. _____

2. This is a task that calls for quickly thinking. _____

3. She came in and smiled friendlily. _____

4. Such is his strength, he pushed the stove clearly through the wall. _____

5. I rightly assumed they'd get into trouble. It serves them rightly.

   _____

6. We go usually to Maine in May. _____

7. She had a nasty fall and could easy have been killed.

   _____

8. It's a fearsome difficult issue, and we have to think clear.

   _____

9. Seeing a child run into the street, the driver stopped shortly.

   _____

10. Obviously, ultimately we will hopefully be fully exonerated if judged fairly and squarely. _____

Comparison

- Adjectives and adverbs have comparative and superlative forms, often formed by adding *-er* and *-est:*

	comparative	superlative
few	fewer	fewest
easy	easier	easiest

- Formation of comparatives and superlatives follows one of two patterns, depending on the number of syllables in the adjective/adverb:

		comparative	superlative
Pattern A	old	older	oldest
Pattern B	cumbersome	more cumbersome	most cumbersome

Words of one syllable follow pattern A:

newer, thinnest, bigger, smallest

Words of three syllables or more follow pattern B:

more extraordinary, most enlightening

Words of two syllables can follow either:

happy	*happier*	*happiest*
often	*more often*	*most often*

- Some words form irregular comparisons:

good	*better*	*best*
bad	*worse*	*worst*
little	*less*	*least*

- Use the comparative to compare one thing to another and the superlative to compare more than two things:

This computer is more economical than that one.

She is the eldest of five sisters.

Trouble Spots

- Using the wrong comparative form:

I have learned by the perfectest method.

As a rule, cows are more tall than sheep.

Exercise

Give the correct comparative form of the words in parentheses:

1. Buying a home is the (important) purchase you will ever make. _____

2. Being an expert time manager, she planned each day (systematic) than the last. _____

3. Many people find e-mail (easy) to use than the telephone.

   _____

4. If you have back problems, this bed will help you sleep (comfortable) than ever. _____

5. Of all the surgeons, Dr. White performs the procedure (successful). _____

6. Here are some ideas for you to do the job (good) than before.

   _____

7. We are looking for a (big, powerful) automobile than our last one. _____

8. In her statement, this witness described the suspect (full) than the others did. _____

9. Thanks to automation, banking is (simple and easy) than ever before. _____

10. I think Jane justified the expenditure (convincing) of all the purchasing committee members. _____

Grammar? No Problem!

All Ready Versus Already

- Several pairs of modifiers sound identical but differ in structure and meaning:

I've already done it. (in advance)

Are we all ready? (totally, or each person, prepared)

Others in this class are:

almost	all most
altogether	all together
always	all ways
anymore	any more
anyone	any one
anytime	any time
anyway	any way
awhile	a while
everyday	every day
everyone	every one
indifferent	in different

Trouble Spots

- Confusing these pairs of modifiers:

Altogether now, sing with me!

She visits me *everyday*.

Exercise

Of the pairs of modifiers enclosed in parentheses, circle the correct form:

1. We have (almost/all most) reached the point of no return.

2. The consignment you ordered is (already/all ready).

3. We tried (always/all ways) to solve the problem, but nothing worked.

4. Take (anyone/any one)—the sandwiches are all the same.

5. If you have (anytime/any time), please stop by the office.

6. I apologized, but she said it didn't matter (anyway/any way).

7. Homelessness and broken families have become (everyday/ every day) problems.

8. Would you like (anymore/any more)? There's plenty in the pot.

9. I counted (everyone/every one), and I assure you not a single box is missing.

10. I sympathize with your situation, even though I am (indifferent/in different) circumstances.

Kind of, Sort of, Type of

- Expressions such as *kind of* and *sort of* function as "softeners" to cushion statements and opinions:

  He was kind of timid for a lion tamer.

  I was sort of angry after reading your note.

  Note: In writing, especially to sound formal, replace *kind of* and *sort of* with *rather, somewhat, relatively,* and so on.

- These expressions also serve as classifiers, along with several others, to show that an item belongs to a class of things:

  this kind of car

  that sort of rumor

  that type of person

  that species of bird

  this variety of rose

Trouble Spots

- Keeping the expression singular when referring to several classes:

  these kind of cars

- Inserting *a* or *an:*

  that type of a person

- slurring the word *of:*

  "I was kinda worried."

Exercise

Correct the "of" expressions in the following sentences:

1. Dear Mr. Smith: We were sort of surprised to receive your shipment so soon.

   _____

2. Unfortunately, Ms. Jones was kind of unwell last week.

   _____

3. What sort of a business are you in?

   _____

4. My daughter likes these kind of candies.

   _____

5. That's kinda expensive for you.

   _____

6. I was sort of like wondering whether to approach you or not.

   _____

7. What kind of a creature did you see?

   _____

8. In response to your inquiry about our services, I would say they are sort of like e-mail.

   _____

9. They were wise to avoid those kind of a problem.

   _____

10. Those type of developments are always very interesting.

    _____

Amount/Number

- Use *number, many,* and *few* if the noun in the sentence can be counted:

  a number of people, many cars, few trains, fewer ships

- When actual numbers are quoted, use *less:*

  less than two hours

- Use *amount, much,* and *little* if the noun cannot be counted:

  an amount of air, much water, little salt, less sand

- When describing amounts/numbers, use *higher/lower* and *larger/smaller,* not *more/less:*

  Crime numbers are higher this year.

  The crowds are smaller than the promoters anticipated.

Trouble Spots

- Using *less* instead of *fewer*

  Less children attend youth clubs these days. (fewer)

- Using *amount* instead of *number*

  A large *amount* of cars collided on the freeway. (number)

- Using *less* with *amount*

  A *less amount* of money is spent on cigarettes these days. (a *smaller amount,* or simply *less money*)

Exercise

Correct the amount/number terms in the sentences below:

1. Pack this equipment using the least possible amount of boxes.

   _____

2. I'm sure we had less rainy days last year.

   _____

3. Fewer than ten years ago there were no malls in this city.

   _____

4. No amount of apologies will make this problem go away.

   _____

5. Due to radioactive contamination, a few people choose to live near the old reactor site.

   _____

6. They were not paying attention, so a little of what I said made any difference.

   _____

7. By the time the will was read, the estate was worth fewer than a million dollars.

   _____

8. The amount of visitors is fewer than this time last year.

   _____

9. Less of us were present, so less of food was eaten.

   _____

10. There's less amount of cars in the city than there were before the transit system.

    _____

 Grammar? No Problem!

Former/Latter

- Indicate a specific word from a pair or list by using *first, former, latter,* and *last.*

  Former and *latter* relate to two items:

  Rice and beans are both nutritional, but I prefer the former. (i.e., rice)

  Many soldiers died in the Revolutionary and Civil Wars, though more in the latter. (i.e., Civil War)

  First and *last* relate to more than two.

  If the choices are Spanish, French, or German, enroll me in the first.

Note: First, last, and latest can also relate to a sequence of events, but be careful not to confuse *last, latter,* and *latest.*

Trouble Spots

- Using the wrong specifier for the number of items in the list:

  Bill, Ben, and Bob arrived, the former in a tuxedo, the latter in jeans.

Exercise

Correct the specifiers in these sentences:

1. Have you heard the last score? The Dodgers are ahead!

2. This is a great job, and it pays better than my latest one.

3. This will probably be grandma's latter new car—she turns one hundred next week.

4. December and January are always cold, but the last is usually colder.

5. They have cherry and banana flavors. I prefer the first.

6. For the former time in her life, she felt appreciated,

7. Of coonhounds, poodles, and pointers, I find the former make the best hunters.

8. I'm calling my lawyer. You haven't heard the latest of this.

9. They run the payroll on the former day of the month.

10. This will be the latter time I'll stay at this disgraceful hotel!

Misplaced Modifiers

- Any change in word order, especially of major sentence elements, can distort or even reverse the meaning:

  Cats catch mice.

  Mice catch cats.

- It is essential to place modifiers beside the sentence elements they modify:

  The woman waved with her handkerchief as the band marched by.

  The woman waved as the band marched by with her handkerchief.

Trouble Spots

- Placing modifiers or major sentence elements in the wrong spot:

  He got the car from a dealer with a worn-out engine.

Exercise

Disentangle the modifiers to rewrite the following sentences:

1. This problem arose because of a delay in spotting errors by the accounting department.

_____

2. Lying unconscious on the field, the doctor examined the quarterback.

_____

3. Personnel hired the person with misgivings.

_____

4. The hang-glider was assembled, hoping that it would not collapse at ten thousand feet.

_____

5. After his trial for perjury, the judge dismissed the case against Billings.

_____

6. By following the rules, the job will be done more efficiently.

_____

7. The research was carried out making certain assumptions about the marketplace.

_____

8. While working on this report, somebody accidentally deleted my files.

_____

9. Most students failed classes for truancy.

_____

10. We got home from a month's vacation last week.

_____

Prepositions

Using Prepositions

- Prepositions show the relationship between a noun or pronoun and some other word in the sentence:

preposition

The book is	*on*	*the table.*
Come	*with*	*me.*

Following are some common prepositions:

about	beside	into	through
above	between	near	to
across	by	next	toward
after	down	of	under
among	during	off	until
around	except	on	up
as	for	out	upon
at	from	over	with
before	in	past	within
behind	inside	since	without
below			

- Certain pairs of prepositions are often confused with each other:

among, between	Among all the prisoners, he was the most remorseful. *(more than two)*
	Please choose between chocolate and vanilla. *(two)*
at, with	The crowd was angry at the final score. *(thing)*
	My husband is angry with our neighbor. *(person)*
beside, besides	The dog walked beside the mail carrier. *(alongside)*
	Besides the inconvenience, we also felt harassed. *(in addition to)*
in, into	We strolled in the museum. *(inside its walls)*
	We strolled into the museum. *(entered)*

- Use prepositions only when necessary:

  Our new house is near the children's school. (Not near to)

Trouble Spots

- Omitting necessary prepositions:

  It's [of] no use to complain.

- Adding unnecessary prepositions:

  He entered into the phone booth.

- Using the wrong preposition:

  She died from pneumonia. (of)

Exercise

Choose the correct preposition from the alternatives in parentheses:

1. I liked the product, but we could not agree (at/on) a price.

2. When Mom saw the mess I made of the car, she got angry (at/with) me.

3. There were many reasons to celebrate (beside/besides) the obvious.

4. If you want to be promoted, you must apply yourself (for/to) the task.

5. Very well, I agree (to/with) your conditions.

6. The lawyer considered the discrepancies (among/between) the witnesses' depositions.

7. A massive retriever plunged (in/into) the lake after the fallen bird.

Add or subtract prepositions as necessary:

8. Where did Jack go to?

9. Do you have a pair scissors I could borrow?

10. We need to discuss about your proposal.

11. The Smiths' house is opposite to ours.

12. I've never seen that type bird before.

13. The engineer was injured when she fell off of the locomotive.

14. He's pleasant and well-educated, but he lacks in experience.

Ending With Prepositions

- Formal style traditionally avoids ending sentences with prepositions, even though it can sometimes lead to clumsy-sounding constructions:

  For whom is the present?

  With what shall I serve the pie?

  You are the cousin to whom I feel closest.

  He reflected on the injustice against which he had fought.

  In casual speech and some informal writing, you might see the following instead:

  Who's the present for?

  What should I serve the pie with?

  You're the cousin I feel closest to.

  He reflected on the injustice he had fought against.

  Though no longer considered essential to good style, avoiding final prepositions when practical to do so is a sign of careful writing.

Trouble Spots:

- Ending sentences with prepositions that have no function:

  Where's the lawnmower at?

  Where are all those pigeons flying to?

Exercise

Rewrite the following to avoid ending with a preposition:

1. Who did you have lunch with?

_____

2. John's bed hasn't been slept in.

_____

3. Which year were you born in?

_____

4. How long have you been waiting for?

_____

5. He's someone I went to school with.

_____

6. Which airline are you flying with?

_____

7. This is the car I told you about.

_____

8. I hate being shouted at.

_____

9. What kind of service are you looking for?

_____

10. Bring me a chair to stand on.

_____

Grammar? No Problem!

Conjunctions

Using Conjunctions

- Conjunctions are words and phrases that link other words, phrases, and clauses.

  They also show how the items they link are logically related:

  fish *and* chips (addition)

  cautious *but* optimistic (contrast)

  sink *or* swim (alternative)

  fired *due to* lateness (cause/effect)

- Some conjunctions work in pairs:

  either/or

  neither/nor

  both/and

  not only/but also

  whether/or

  The first element in these pairs positions right before whatever they serve to join:

  Either finish your homework or go to bed.

  I have neither the time nor the patience to balance this checkbook.

  The child wanted both a hamburger and a hot dog.

  Jessica Tandy was not only a fine actress, but also quite charming.

  Whether it rains or shines, the runners will complete the marathon.

Trouble Spots

- Using the wrong conjunction and disrupting the logic of the sentence:

  Although the mountains get a lot of snow, the ski season is long.

Exercise

Choose the correct conjunction from the alternatives in parentheses:

1. Progress has been slow; (therefore/however), there is some hope.

2. I need a hammer (and/or) some nails to hang those pictures.

3. We could book a hotel. (Also/On the other hand), it would be nice to camp.

4. Expecting to camp, we took a tent (as well as/rather than) sleeping bags.

5. (Even if/Even though) they do make it tonight, it will be too late to go out.

6. (In order that/Because) the presentation would succeed, they hired a PR consultant.

7. I will not agree to these measures (unless/even if) the boss gives me no choice.

8. Let's wait in the lounge (while/until) they arrive.

9. I offered them a ride, (and/but) they preferred to walk.

10. (Not only/Neither) do I believe them (but also/nor) could I ever trust them again.

Grammar and Style

Confusing Word Pairs

- Certain word pairs, even though common, often cause confusion. Following are a few:

  as / like

  bi- / semi-

  bring / take

  compose / comprise

  disinterested / uninterested

  flaunt / flout

  imply / infer

  learn / teach

  regard / regards

  than / then

Though each has a distinct meaning and application, it's sometimes useful to create memory devices for yourself to stay out of usage trouble:

I use a pen with my stationery; I stand perfectly still when I'm stationary.

Trouble Spots

- Making the wrong choice from pairs of confusibles:

  The mastiff stood taller then the Shetland pony.

  With regards to losing weight, it's the exercise that I hate.

Exercise

Choose the correct alternative from the word pairs in parentheses:

1. With (regard/regards) to your request, the shipment is on its way.

2. As a (disinterested/uninterested) party, I would advise you to accept the offer.

3. Your comments seem to (imply/infer) that you disagree.

4. The demonstrators (flaunted/flouted) the authorities by taking to the streets after curfew.

5. The complex is (composed/comprised) of homes, gardens, and stores.

6. The (bi-/semi-) annual reviews are conducted December 1 and June 1.

7. (As/Like) I told you, there is no school today.

8. That's a clever trick! Could you (learn/teach) it to me?

9. If you're going to Mary's house, (bring/take) these with you.

10. This blouse came cleaner (than/then) I ever thought possible.

Redundancy

- *Redundancy* comes from a Latin word meaning "repetition." A redundant (unnecessary) word repeats something already said:

  advance planning

  basic essentials

  combine together

  consensus of opinion

  past experience

  leftover surplus

Trouble Spots

- Adding unnecessary words, usually for the sake of emphasis or attempted clarity:

  at a later date

  my personal opinion

  very true

Exercise

Eliminate the redundancies in these sentences:

1. Ms. Smith can't see you at this moment in time.

   _____

2. We waited for a period of one week.

   _____

3. At this point, the two highways merged together.

   _____

4. Never ever think of returning back.

   _____

5. This is a very unique piece of jewelry.

   _____

6. In actual fact, the documents have already been signed.

   _____

7. The end result of the process was stalemate.

   _____

8. These findings are the complete opposite of what we expected.

   _____

9. We had no other alternative than to close the factory.

   _____

10. Past experience tells us that such mistakes can be avoided.

   _____

Parallel Constructions

- Items listed in a series should all be the same part of speech or grammatical form (i.e., parallel constructions):

noun + noun + noun

Doreen is an expert gardener, cook, and pilot.

verb + verb + verb

Bill looked at the contract, spoke with the client, and found no conflict.

Trouble Spots

- Using nonparallel constructions:

We'll be there, rain, snow, wind, or hailing.

The librarian sorted books, tapes, and straightened the magazines.

Exercise

Change the following into parallel constructions:

1. To be or isn't—that is the question.

2. I know you will find the exercise a healthy experience and enjoy it.

3. They chose sailing rather than to fly to Mexico.

4. Good health is like having wealth.

5. We guarantee quality, a personal, service, and integrity.

6. The induction ceremony was mysterious and an honor.

7. The new vehicle is economical, fast, and it runs very smoothly.

8. The cat is small, gray, Siamese, and with yellow eyes.

9. Management has already started to operate more efficiently and employing scientific methods.

10. The book covers dealing with employees, how to manage in crisis, and the discovery of self.

Mangled Misstatements

- Figures of speech such as proverbs, clichés, idioms, and metaphors can add color, life, and even humor to language as long as they're incorporated accurately as well as effectively:

  The slogan for the rubber raft company was, "You can lead a horse to water, but you can't make him sink!"

Trouble Spots

- Using figures of speech that are widely recognizable (which is what gives them their power) in an inappropriate way:

  time to swallow the bullet

  grab the bull by the tail

  flog a dead horse to death

  listen with a forked ear

Exercise

Complete the proverbs correctly:

1. A stitch in time <u>saves a lot of trouble.</u>

2. Don't kill the goose that lays <u>all the money.</u>

3. Don't waste your time: you're <u>whipping a lame mount.</u>

4. Every cloud has a <u>happy ending.</u>

5. People who live in glass houses shouldn't <u>criticize others.</u>

6. If at first you don't succeed, <u>have another go.</u>

7. The early bird <u>has a distinct time advantage.</u>

8. Fools rush in where <u>more sensible people would exercise caution.</u>

9. Least said, <u>least problems afterwards.</u>

10. Don't put all your eggs in <u>a place where they're all at risk.</u>

Answer Key

Parts of Speech Exercise, p. 4

1. pronoun

2. noun

3. auxiliary verb

4. adverb

5. main verb

6. article

7. adjective

8. adjective

9. & 15. conjunction

10. adjective

11. noun

12. adjective

13. & 17. preposition

14. noun

16. adjective

18. noun

Subject-Verb-Object Exercise, p. 7

1. pattern D
2. pattern E
3. pattern A
4. variation b
5. variation a
6. variation c
7. fragment
8. pattern B
9. pattern C
10. variation d

Proper Nouns Exercise, p. 12

1. Stanford, Palo Alto, California
2. rivers, lakes, streams, fish
3. Richard, Trout Lake, Hanukkah
4. Manhattan, Hudson River, East River, New York Bay
5. *Parks and Gardens,* Doctor Hans Helmut Gruendaum
6. north side of town, father and brother
7. German-speaking, Swiss Catholic
8. banks, branches, malls, main streets
9. high school, sciences, bachelor of commerce degree
10. Liberty Bell, Pennsylvania State Assembly, State House, Philadelphia

Collective Nouns Exercise, p. 15

1. it will honor
2. has in fact
3. serve its membership
4. Human Resources has
5. My family is
6. The board, which is
7. have come to their decision
8. all of which, is going wild
9. has a better chance
10. it has decided to

Compound Nouns Exercise, p. 18

1. printout
2. cutbacks
3. nitty-gritty
4. merry-go-round
5. leftovers
6. carryings-on
7. crackdown
8. hideaway
9. goody-goody
10. stand-in

Plurals Exercise, p. 21

1. elves, witches
2. heroes, logos
3. wolves, calves
4. lice, teeth
5. species, geese
6. headquarters, barracks
7. villages, ferries
8. Women, children
9. watches, quartzes
10. copies, policies

Plurals From Other Languages Exercise, p. 23

1. analyses, data
2. matrices, appendices
3. alumni, prognoses
4. media, stimuli
5. theses, hypotheses
6. cacti, oases
7. phenomena, formulae
8. bacteria, vertebrae
9. criteria, memoranda
10. bases, diagnoses

Possessives Exercise, p. 25

1. Mr. and Mrs. Jones's sons

2. women's issues

3. Paris's parks and gardens

4. the ferries' captains

5. the investors' interests

6. the attorneys' offices

7. the executives' decision

8. Arkansas' hills

9. the sheep's feet

10. Alice's restaurant

11. Mr. Rogers's neighborhood

12. the men's locker room

13. California's highways

14. Max's friends

15. the corps's soldiers

Compound Noun Possessives Exercise, p. 27

1. the eyewitness's testimony
2. the brothers-in-law's wives
3. the congresswomen's meeting
4. a culture-vultures' gathering
5. a go-between's duties
6. the passersby's comments
7. a layabout's life
8. the attorneys-at-law's offices
9. an old so-and-so's luck
10. the president-elect's speech

Pronoun and Antecedent Exercise, p. 31

1. has received his orders
2. know how to take care of their vehicles
3. her mother had a cold
4. to lose his promotion
5. because medicine is more demanding
6. launched their new software
7. where Pete caught a train
8. the Blues are a great team
9. as it was supposed to
10. since the profits created new jobs

Personal Pronouns Exercise, p. 34

1. and bring one for me
2. Mary and I
3. to Bert and me
4. Before giving
5. Julie . . . herself . . . she
6. It was I
7. put self-interest first
8. Between you and me
9. Bob, Ted, Carol, and I
10. your and your sister's lives
11. helped himself
12. its owner
13. yourselves . . . ourselves
14. He and she were . . . doing themselves
15. people like them . . . all of us

Relative Pronouns Exercise, p. 36

1. who can be trusted
2. People who
3. The dog that
4. which surprised everybody
5. who always causes
6. which I told you
7. that is too sad
8. Enterprise, which
9. whom you suggested
10. that first reported

Who/Whom Exercise, p. 38

1. whom
2. whoever
3. who . . . who
4. whom
5. who
6. whomever . . . whom . . . who
7. who . . . whom . . . whom
8. whom
9. Who . . . whom
10. Whom . . . whomever

Who's/Whose Exercise, p. 40

1. Whose
2. Who's
3. Whose
4. Who's
5. Whose
6. Whose
7. Who's
8. Who's
9. Whose
10. Who's

Subject-Verb Agreement Exercise, p. 43

1. is
2. is
3. is
4. are . . . are
5. is
6. are
7. is
8. is
9. are
10. is

Tenses Exercise, p. 46

1. present simple . . . future perfect progressive

2. present perfect

3. future progressive

4. past simple

5. future perfect . . . present simple

6. present perfect progressive

7. past progressive . . . past simple

8. future simple . . . future simple

9. present progressive

10. past perfect . . . past perfect

Sequence of Tenses Exercise, p. 48

1. I would see you

2. and did you also know

3. he said he was going

4. less interested I became

5. they saw a stranger who asked them

6. and wondered where he had been

7. brother was playing . . . sister was singing

8. we eat it

9. it started to howl

10. I'd never heard

Parts of Verbs Exercise, p. 50

1. I've never sung

2. I shrank

3. He's run

4. are frozen . . . is frozen . . . are frozen

5. never ridden

6. never spoken

7. He's written

8. they'd never gone

9. We've given

10. they had shown

Passives Exercise, p. 52

1. She was seriously injured in the accident.

2. I was being followed by someone.

3. Who is going to be told about the reorganization?

4. Everything will have been finished (will be finished) by Friday.

5. I knew why I had been chosen.

6. We intend to replace you.

7. They expected you earlier.

8. The principal will discipline them.

9. The personnel manager has notified Robert of his dismissal.

10. The gang will have given Suzie her present by now.

Conditionals Exercise, p. 54

1. If you had not called

2. she would have passed

3. if they had had

4. The town would have been . . . if she had been

5. If you had asked me (Had you asked me)

6. if I brought a partner

7. would have, could have, or should have

8. If he had been . . . you would never have

9. we would have completely finished

10. they would not have gone

Subjunctives Exercise, p. 56

1. that the information be provided

2. that you come at the earliest . . .

3. that he do the work

4. He wishes he were going

5. that we be allowed

6. If only it were

7. that Briggs remain in prison

8. that they be allowed a pay increase

9. that the court award

10. Peace be with you.

Split Infinitives Exercise, p. 58

1. We tried to reassemble the parts carefully
2. Try to exercise, if you can, two or three
3. Gradually they began to pick up
4. to question thoroughly the people
5. to supervise the renovations personally
6. to be checked meticulously
7. to be fed carrots constantly
8. gather the information rapidly
9. to find even one person
10. We really want to understand

Shall/Will Exercise, p. 60

1. Will
2. should
3. would
4. Would
5. Shall
6. should
7. would
8. would
9. would
10. will

Can/May Exercise, p. 62

1. might
2. May
3. May
4. could
5. could . . . could
6. could
7. might
8. might have been
9. could
10. might

Lay/Lie Exercise, p. 64

1. laid
2. Lie
3. raised
4. risen
5. laying
6. lay
7. raised
8. laid
9. lay
10. raised . . . lay

Negatives Exercise, p. 66

1. never had any
2. didn't have any
3. hardly ever comes
4. don't have any
5. never has any
6. the books or the stationery
7. unable to give us any
8. Bill was not aware
9. I can't find either . . . or
10. Neither trucks nor cars are

Contractions Exercise, p. 68

1. I'd had

2. You've been

3. She'd be

4. He'll see

5. It's a

6. We're in

7. We'd heard

8. It mightn't

9. There's . . . there's

10. If we'd been . . . there'd be

11. Don't think you're

12. If you couldn't . . . why didn't

13. Shouldn't you be asking why they weren't

14. I wouldn't worry, they'll

15. I can't, I won't, and I shan't

Adjectives Versus Adverbs Exercise, p. 71

1. adjective
2. adverb
3. adverb
4. adjective
5. adverb
6. adjective
7. adverb
8. adverb
9. adverb
10. adjective

Order of Adjectives Exercise, p. 73

1. a small brown German beer bottle
2. the great green greasy Limpopo River
3. the delightful little old Pasadena lady
4. a massive round oak dining table
5. long thin flexible steel poles
6. a delicious long cool refreshing drink
7. white Italian leather dancing shoes
8. large fresh farm duck eggs
9. a remote little old rustic cottage
10. that splendid big red Brazilian parrot

Compound Adjectives Exercise, p. 75

1. a never-to-be-forgotten moment
2. a three-dimensional representation
3. an on-and-off affair
4. off-the-record information
5. point-of-sale transactions
6. a once-in-a-lifetime experience
7. a cause-and-effect relationship
8. 24-hour-a-day service
9. a ten-million-mile journey
10. a dog-and-pony show

Use of Adverbs Exercise, p. 77

1. some really good deals
2. for quick thinking
3. gave a friendly smile
4. clear through the wall
5. It serves them right.
6. We usually go
7. could easily have been killed
8. fearsomely difficult . . . think clearly
9. the driver stopped short
10. We hope to be exonerated if judged fairly.

Comparison Exercise, p. 80

1. the most important
2. more systematically
3. easier
4. more comfortably
5. most successfully
6. better
7. bigger, more powerful
8. more fully
9. simpler and easier
10. (the) most convincingly

All Ready Versus Already Exercise, p. 82

1. almost
2. all ready
3. all ways
4. any one
5. any time
6. anyway
7. everyday
8. any more
9. every one
10. in different

Kind of, Sort of, Type of Exercise, p. 84

1. We were surprised

2. Ms. Jones was unwell

3. What sort of business

4. this kind/these kinds of candy

5. That's kind of expensive.

6. I was wondering

7. What kind of creature

8. they are similar to e-mail

9. those kinds of problems/that kind of problem

10. Those types of developments

Amount/Number Exercise, p. 86

1. as few boxes as possible

2. fewer rainy days

3. less than ten years ago

4. no amount of apologizing

5. few people choose

6. little of what I said

7. less than a million

8. The number of visitors is lower/smaller

9. Fewer . . . less food

10. There are fewer cars

Former/Latter Exercise, p. 88

1. the latest score

2. my last one

3. last new car

4. the latter

5. the former

6. For the first time

7. I find the first make

8. You haven't heard the last

9. the first day of the month

10. this will be the last time

Misplaced Modifiers Exercise, p. 90

1. a delay by the accounting department in spotting

2. The doctor examined the quarterback, who was lying

3. hired the person, although they had misgivings

4. and the pilot hoped

5. after his trial, Billings's case was dismissed

6. By following the rules, you will do the job

7. The research was carried out on the basis of certain assumptions

8. While I was working on this report, somebody accidentally deleted

9. failed their classes because of truancy

10. We got home last week from

Using Prepositions Exercise, p. 94

1. on
2. with
3. besides
4. to
5. to
6. among
7. into
8. Where did Jack go?
9. a pair of scissors
10. discuss your proposal
11. their house is opposite ours
12. that type of bird
13. fell off the locomotive
14. he lacks experience

Ending With Prepositions Exercise, p. 96

1. With whom did you have lunch?
2. John hasn't slept in his bed.
3. In which year were you born?
4. For how long have you been waiting?
5. I went to school with him.
6. With which airline are you flying?
7. This is the car I mentioned.
8. I hate it when you shout at me.
9. What kind of service are you seeking?
10. Bring me a chair on which to stand.

Using Conjunctions Exercise, p. 100

1. however
2. and
3. On the other hand
4. as well as
5. Even if
6. In order that
7. unless
8. until
9. but
10. Neither . . . nor

Confusing Word Pairs Exercise, p. 103

1. regard
2. disinterested
3. imply
4. flouted
5. composed
6. semi-
7. As
8. teach
9. take
10. than

Redundancy Exercise, p. 105

1. Ms. Smith can't see you now.
2. We waited for a week.
3. At this point, the highways merged.
4. Never think of returning.
5. This is a unique piece of jewelry.
6. The documents have already been signed.
7. The result of the process was stalemate.
8. These findings are the opposite of what we expected.
9. We had no alternative but to close the factory.
10. Experience tells us that such mistakes can be avoided.

Parallel Constructions Exercise, p. 107

1. To be or not to be
2. a healthy and enjoyable experience
3. sailing . . . flying
4. Good health is like wealth.
5. quality, personal service, and integrity
6. a mystery and an honor
7. economical, fast, and smooth running
8. a small, gray, yellow-eyed Siamese
9. to operate . . . and employ
10. dealing with employees, managing in a crisis, and discovering the self

Managed Misstatements Exercise, p. 109

1. A stitch in time <u>saves nine.</u>

2. Don't kill the goose that lays <u>the golden egg.</u>

3. Don't waste your time: you're <u>flogging a dead horse.</u>

4. Every cloud has a <u>silver lining.</u>

5. People who live in glass houses shouldn't <u>throw stones.</u>

6. If at first you don't succeed, <u>try and try again.</u>

7. The early bird <u>catches the worm.</u>

8. Fools rush in where <u>angels fear to tread.</u>

9. Least said, <u>soonest mended.</u>

10. Don't put all your eggs in <u>one basket.</u>

Bibliography and Suggested Reading

Axtell, Roger. *Do's and Taboos of Using English Around the World.* New York: John Wiley & Sons, 1995.

Barzun, Jacques. *A Word or Two Before You Go.* Middleton, CT: Wesleyan University Press, 1986.

Booher, Dianna. *Good Grief, Good Grammar.* New York: Facts On File Publications, 1988.

Celce-Murcia, Marianne, and Diane Larsen-Freeman. *The Grammar Book.* Rowley, MA: Newbury House, 1983.

Chalker, Sylvia, and Edmund Wiener. *The Oxford Dictionary of English Grammar.* Oxford: Clarnedon Press, 1994.

Davies, David. *English for Commerce.* Englewood Cliffs, NJ: Prentice-Hall, 1990.

Gowers, Earnest. *The Complete Plain Words.* London: HMSO, 1986.

Kramer, Melinda, Glenn Leggett, and David C. Mead. *Prentice Hall Handbook for Writers.* Englewood Cliffs, NJ: Prentice-Hall, 1995.

Lindsell-Roberts, Sheryl (ed.). *Merriam Webster's Secretarial Handbook.* Springfield, MA: Merriam Webster, 1993.

Mish, Frederick C. (ed.). *The New Merriam-Webster Dictionary.*
Springfield, MA: Merriam Webster, 1989.

Sabin, William A. *The Gregg Reference Manual, 7th ed.* Westerville,
OH: Glencoe, 1995.

Safire, William, and Leonard Safir (eds.). *Good Advice on Writing.*
New York: Simon & Schuster, 1992.

Strunk, William, and E.B. White. *Elements of Style.* New York:
Macmillan, 1979.

Thomson, A. J., and A.V. Martinet. *A Practical English Grammar.*
New York: Oxford University Press, 1990.

Zinsser, William. *On Writing Well.* New York: Harper Collins,
1976.

Available From SkillPath Publications

Self-Study Sourcebooks

Climbing the Corporate Ladder: What You Need to Know and Do to Be a Promotable Person *by Barbara Pachter and Marjorie Brody*

Coping With Supervisory Nightmares: 12 Common Nightmares of Leadership and What You Can Do About Them *by Michael and Deborah Singer Dobson*

Defeating Procrastination: 52 Fail-Safe Tips for Keeping Time on Your Side *by Marlene Caroselli, Ed.D.*

Discovering Your Purpose *by Ivy Haley*

Going for the Gold: Winning the Gold Medal for Financial Independence *by Lesley D. Bissett, CFP*

Having Something to Say When You Have to Say Something: The Art of Organizing Your Presentation *by Randy Horn*

Info-Flood: How to Swim in a Sea of Information Without Going Under *by Marlene Caroselli, Ed.D.*

The Innovative Secretary *by Marlene Caroselli, Ed.D.*

Letters & Memos: Just Like That! *by Dave Davies*

Mastering the Art of Communication: Your Keys to Developing a More Effective Personal Style *by Michelle Fairfield Poley*

Organized for Success! 95 Tips for Taking Control of Your Time, Your Space, and Your Life *by Nanci McGraw*

A Passion to Lead! How to Develop Your Natural Leadership Ability *by Michael Plumstead*

P.E.R.S.U.A.D.E.: Communication Strategies That Move People to Action *by Marlene Caroselli, Ed.D.*

Productivity Power: 250 Great Ideas for Being More Productive *by Jim Temme*

Promoting Yourself: 50 Ways to Increase Your Prestige, Power, and Paycheck *by Marlene Caroselli, Ed.D.*

Proof Positive: How to Find Errors Before They Embarrass You *by Karen L. Anderson*

Risk-Taking: 50 Ways to Turn Risks Into Rewards *by Marlene Caroselli, Ed.D. and David Harris*

Speak Up and Stand Out: How to Make Effective Presentations *by Nanci McGraw*

Stress Control: How You Can Find Relief From Life's Daily Stress *by Steve Bell*

The Technical Writer's Guide *by Robert McGraw*

Total Quality Customer Service: How to Make It Your Way of Life *by Jim Temme*

Write It Right! A Guide for Clear and Correct Writing *by Richard Andersen and Helene Hinis*

Your Total Communication Image *by Janet Signe Olson, Ph.D.*

Handbooks

The ABC's of Empowered Teams: Building Blocks for Success *by Mark Towers*

Assert Yourself! Developing Power-Packed Communication Skills to Make Your Points Clearly, Confidently, and Persuasively *by Lisa Contini*

Breaking the Ice: How to Improve Your On-the-Spot Communication Skills *by Deborah Shouse*

The Care and Keeping of Customers: A Treasury of Facts, Tips, and Proven Techniques for Keeping Your Customers Coming BACK! *by Roy Lantz*

Challenging Change: Five Steps for Dealing With Change *by Holly DeForest and Mary Steinberg*

Dynamic Delegation: A Manager's Guide for Active Empowerment *by Mark Towers*

Every Woman's Guide to Career Success *by Denise M. Dudley*

Grammar? No Problem! *by Dave Davies*

Great Openings and Closings: 28 Ways to Launch and Land Your Presentations With Punch, Power, and Pizazz *by Mari Pat Varga*

Hiring and Firing: What Every Manager Needs to Know *by Marlene Caroselli, Ed.D. with Laura Wyeth, Ms.Ed.*

How to Be a More Effective Group Communicator: Finding Your Role and Boosting Your Confidence in Group Situations *by Deborah Shouse*

How to Deal With Difficult People *by Paul Friedman*

Learning to Laugh at Work: The Power of Humor in the Workplace *by Robert McGraw*

Making Your Mark: How to Develop a Personal Marketing Plan for Becoming More Visible and More Appreciated at Work *by Deborah Shouse*

Meetings That Work *by Marlene Caroselli, Ed.D.*

The Mentoring Advantage: How to Help Your Career Soar to New Heights *by Pam Grout*

Minding Your Business Manners: Etiquette Tips for Presenting Yourself Professionally in Every Business Situation *by Marjorie Brody and Barbara Pachter*

Misspeller's Guide *by Joel and Ruth Schroeder*

Motivation in the Workplace: How to Motivate Workers to Peak Performance and Productivity *by Barbara Fielder*

NameTags Plus: Games You Can Play When People Don't Know What to Say *by Deborah Shouse*

Networking: How to Creatively Tap Your People Resources *by Colleen Clarke*

New & Improved! 25 Ways to Be More Creative and More Effective *by Pam Grout*

Power Write! A Practical Guide to Words That Work *by Helene Hinis*

The Power of Positivity: Eighty ways to energize your life *by Joel and Ruth Schroeder*

Putting Anger to Work For You *by Ruth and Joel Schroeder*

Reinventing Your Self: 28 Strategies for Coping With Change *by Mark Towers*

Saying "No" to Negativity: How to Manage Negativity in Yourself, Your Boss, and Your Co-Workers *by Zoie Kaye*

The Supervisor's Guide: The Everyday Guide to Coordinating People and Tasks *by Jerry Brown and Denise Dudley, Ph.D.*

Taking Charge: A Personal Guide to Managing Projects and Priorities *by Michal E. Feder*

Treasure Hunt: 10 Stepping Stones to a New and More Confident You! *by Pam Grout*

A Winning Attitude: How to Develop Your Most Important Asset! *by Michelle Fairfield Poley*

For more information, call 1-800-873-7545.

Notes

Notes

Notes

Notes

Notes

Notes

Notes

Notes

Notes

Notes